Due to the more difficult math challenges, a ruler and
a triangle came to the desk. Triangle loved to measure
angles, while, for Ruler, straight lines were the most
beautiful thing in the world. When he could guide the pencil...

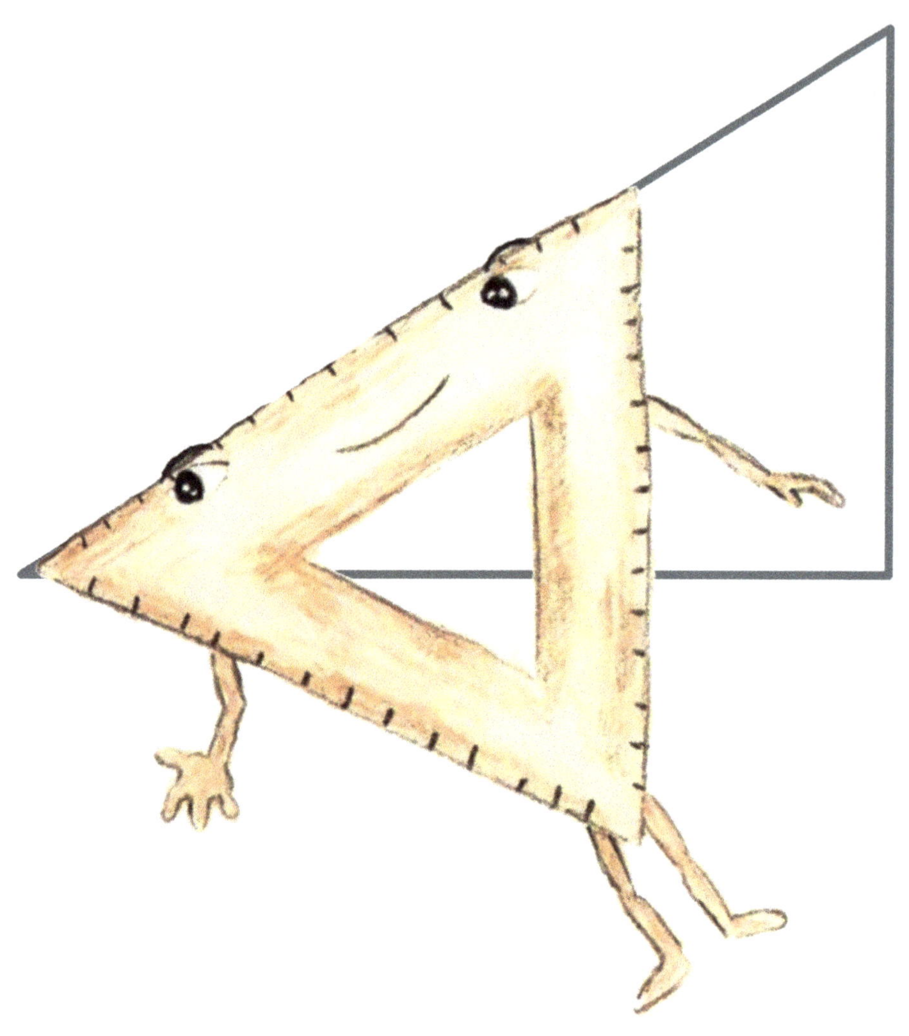

… Ruler tingled all the way from his head to the tips of his toes. For Pencil, this felt strange. He thought that straight strokes were boring, and angles didn't interest him at all. Pencil dreamed of something else while writing the numbers.

First published in German in 2021 by BooksonDemand
This paperback edition published in 2022

© 2021 Christian-Lothar Ludwig
Illustratior: © 2019 Larry Stevenson
Translator: Christian-Lothar Ludwig
Editor: Gayle Green

ISBN: 978-3-9824397-0-9

Printed by:
Ingram Book Group LLC
One Ingram Blvd
LA Vergne, TN 37086, USA

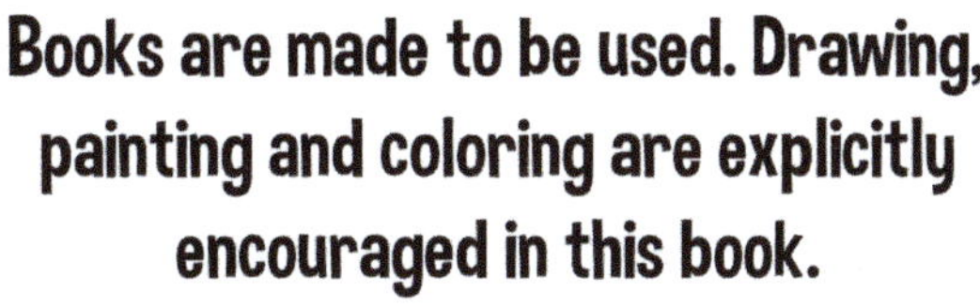

Books are made to be used. Drawing, painting and coloring are explicitly encouraged in this book.

8+3=11   5-3=2   3+6=9

1+2=3   19-9=10   17-9=8

11+7=18   1+2=3

25-12=13   8+7=15

12-4=8

18-7=11   5+9=14

13+7=20   17+4=21

17-4=13   5+19=24

1+9=10

Once upon a time, a Pencil came to a desk to calculate and solve mathematic problems in an exercise book. He ran across the paper, pressed down his tip to make symbols and numbers appear, and then calculated the result.

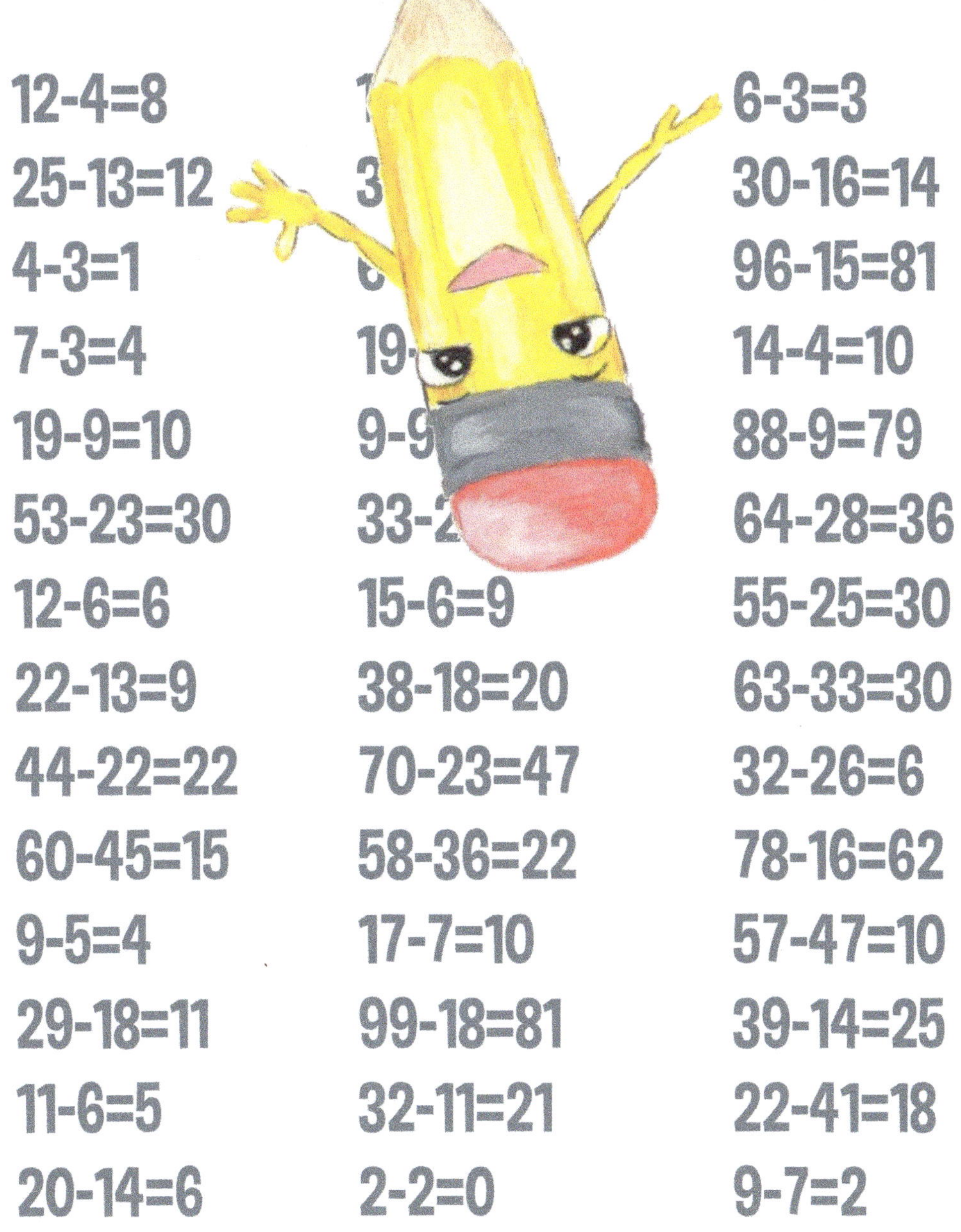

Back in the stationery shop, the other pencils had talked about 'it'. For him, a math pencil, it was probably absurd, but the others had mentioned that 'it' felt magical. This made him curious, so he wanted to try 'it' - he wanted to dance, because that was supposedly how sketches originated on paper.

Pencil had never drawn before and was afraid. If he tried to dance, he might fall or break his tip. One day, however, when he opened the exercise book to calculate something, he discovered a scrawled black sketch.

Pencil didn't know who had scribbled in the exercise book, but he knew that even a math pencil could do better. But, instead of trying it or solving the math problems like he was supposed to, he only stared at the sketch. The strokes were interesting and tempting, but he knew he was made to write numbers only. Nevertheless, following each new arithmetic problem solved …

2x2=4	2x5=10	4x6=24
3x5=15	5x5=25	9x5=45
6x4=24	9x8=72	5x3=15
2x9=18	5x7=35	8x7=42
8x5=40	7x6=42	10x6=60
3x8=24	8x8=64	12x12=144
7x7=49	1x7=7	1x9=9
9x4=	2x7=14	9x7=63
5x4=	8x6=48	5x6=30
3x3=	6x6=36	3x6=18
10x10=	9x5=45	7x5=35
10x4=40	4x4=16	2x2=4
8x2=16	3x2=6	5x2=10

... Pencil contemplated dancing a little more. Then, while calculating, he gathered all his courage and after he had finished his tasks, he hopped onto the neighboring page and took a deep breath. He started dancing and ... doodling! In the corners he staggered, on a straight line he almost slipped, and while shading he hit his head on the table. Nevertheless, Pencil cheered with joy as he finished his first sketch.

When Triangle heard the cheering and noticed Pencil scribbling, she came running and declared in a know-it-all-manner that grey pencils were made for doing math, because that was what Ruler had said. Triangle hurriedly summoned Eraser to remove the drawing immediately. Fortunately, Pencil managed to turn the page in time.

12:4=3   28:7=4   15:5=3
24:6=4   25:5=5   26:13=2
44:11=4   4:2=2   144:12=12
99:33=3   8:2=4   80:8=10
18:9=2   20:4=5   56:7=8
15:5=3   50-25=2   64:8=8
81:9=9   12:6=2   12:[illegible]
22:2=11   39:13=3   [illegible]
44:22=2   100:10=10   [illegible]2:3
60:4=15   60:30=2   [illegible]5=2
8:2=4   70:7=10   30:3=10
30:6=5   77:7=11   48:6=8
10:2=5   12:3=4   45:15=3
14:14=1   20:5=4

Creating that little sketch changed Pencil. He had enjoyed wiggling across the paper and was already looking forward to doing it again. So, before doing his next math problem, he leapt and then somersaulted, and before he had even touched the page, he had thought up a new dance.

With sophisticated dance steps, a tree emerged. The sketch was far better than the crooked house he had drawn previously and this made Pencil happy. While dancing, he forgot the sometimes difficult arithmetic problems he had to solve. Instead of calculating results, he now preferred to think about what could be done with his drawings. That's how the idea of creating a book emerged. However, the one with the grey tip did not know how to think up a story …

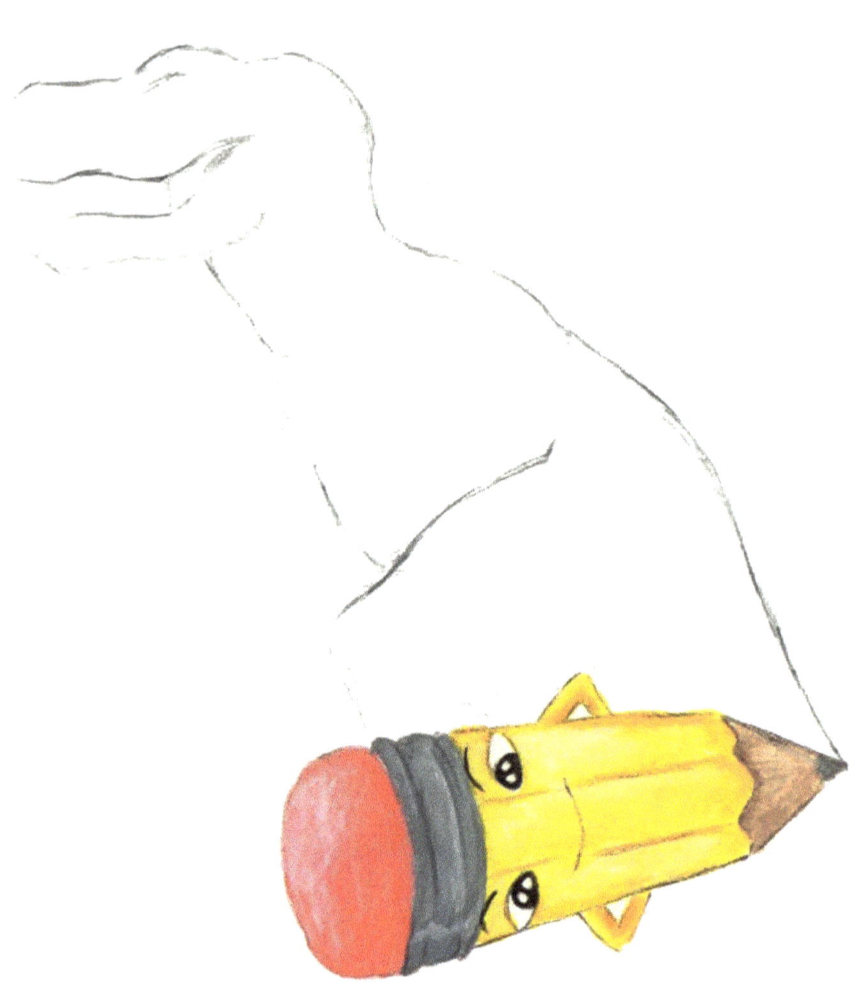

… and how to start a book was also a mystery to him. The most he could do was think up dances. While he was contemplating this dilemma, he created a new sketch that looked like a friendly monster. His friends didn't like this at all.

They laughed at Pencil, as they thought his dances were wobbly and his drawings weird. They said he should stick to writing numbers and drawing straight lines. After all, what did he want with pointless scribbles that would end up somewhere in the pile of papers on the desk anyway?

Pencil told them about his dream to dance drawings to create a book. It would be for children and would make them laugh. Of course, he still had to practice, but he was sure he had talent. To show his progress, he drew himself with strong arms and a cap instead of the rubber hat he usually wore.

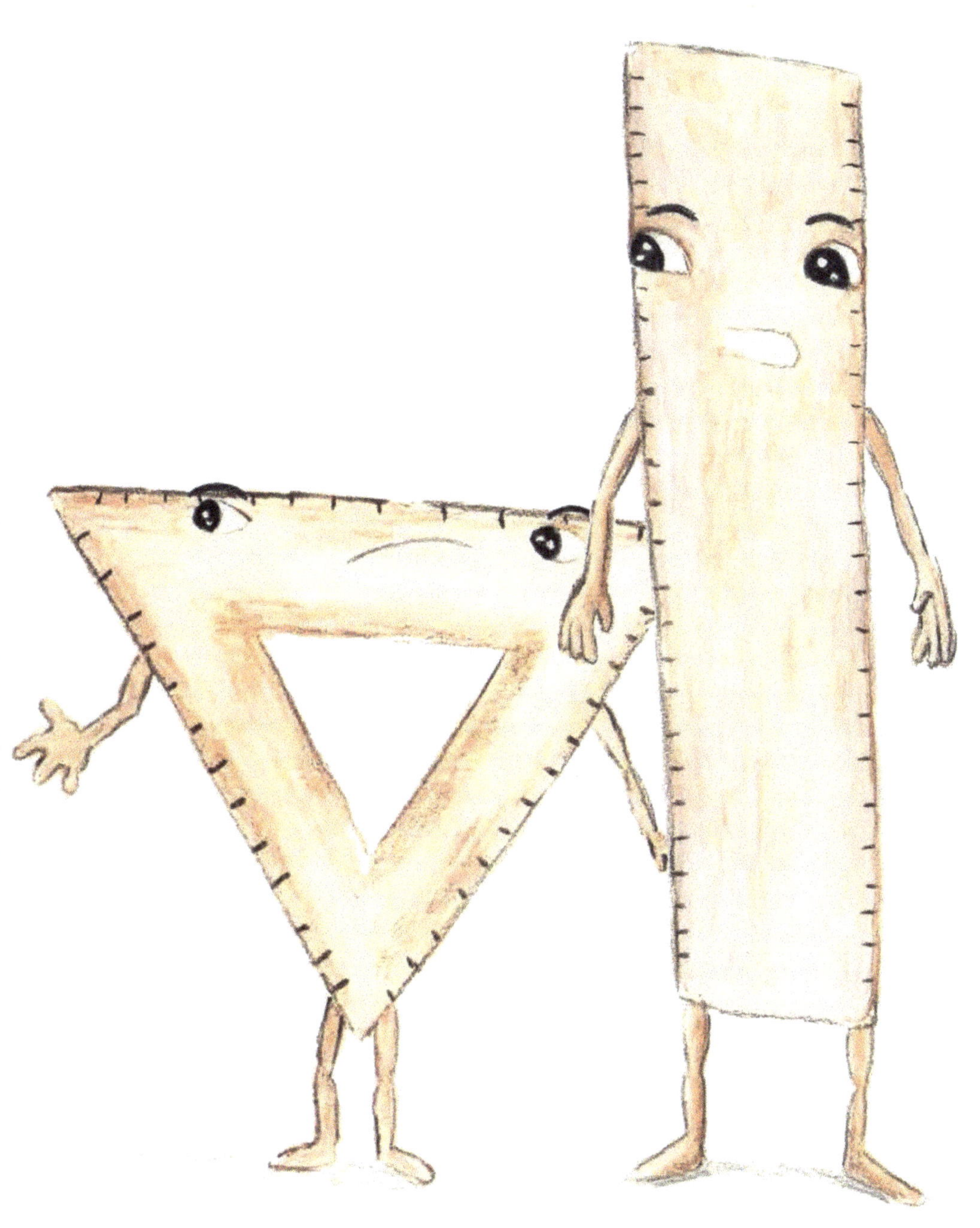

Immediately, laughter echoed throughout the exercise book. How could one single pencil make a book? That was far too much and futile work, hissed Ruler. Triangle added that Grey was needed for math homework, which was more important. That made Pencil ponder.

He knew that homework and extra math exercises had a purpose, but couldn't that be done on scratch paper? All he wanted to do from now on in the math exercise book was dance and draw. While he marched thoughtfully back and forth on the page, he accidentally drew some lines that Ruler saw.

You could hear loud nagging from the other side of the page. Ruler didn't like the odd scribbles at all and told Pencil he should stop his crooked mischief. He said Pencil could never be part of a book. After all, math was all you needed and it always took place in an exercise book, not a real book.

Ruler's unkind words offended Pencil. He didn't want to start in an exercise book and draw in it if it could never become a real book. But he also didn't want to practice much math anymore. Doing just homework was sufficient. Disappointed, he tried his dances on scratch paper in the farthest corner of the desk and wondered whether his wooden friends should really be his yardstick.

Pencil had always believed that friends should support you and your dreams, even if they found them strange. He drew on countless sheets of scratch paper before he regained his courage and got over his disappointment. When he finally returned to the exercise book, Glue Stick had stuck two pages together. Pencil did not want his tip smeared with glue and so he turned the page before starting something big.

He danced a giant's dance. But when he checked his work, he realized that his drawings were still missing something, as children probably wanted to see colorful pictures, not grey ones. But for that, he needed the help of the crayons who lived almost forgotten at the back of the drawer.

He invited them to color two pages in the exercise book. The crayons were a bit rusty and since they hardly came out of the drawer, they had had little practice and then only ever made colored rainbows. However, while coloring the paper, a joyful squealing sound could be heard, and depending on the color, the squeals were of different volumes and pitches.

When Pencil asked if they wanted to help him, he was met with a harsh tone. The coloreds wanted nothing to do with a pencil that was yellow on the outside and grey on the inside. Besides, grey pictures looked gloomy; coloring was for felt-tip pens and real coloring pencils didn't need sketches anyway.

Ruler agreed and claimed that the rain cloud color was only meant for numbers. Besides, at most, the touch-up pen wanted to see colorful elephants, but for that he only needed to sniff the smelly Glue Stick. Pencil got sad. All he wanted to do was create something beautiful for children, but everyone seemed to be against him. Deep in thought, he rolled over to the next page.

There, bored Pencil rolled from the top of the page to the bottom and back. Only when he heard a deep voice did he straighten up. He caught sight of the black pencil standing waiting on the other side. He had been watching the happenings in the exercise book from his place in the pencil case since Pencil had danced his first sketch. And now he wanted to talk to him.

Black had come to the desk in the same box as the other crayons. However, he immediately ended up in the pencil case and had been there ever since. The crayons didn't like him because he wasn't a colorful color. He looked dark like the night and coloring and the color black just didn't go together.

Black told Pencil that he wanted to dance too. He said he couldn't sketch, that he had already tried that, but he could draw inside lines very well. Pencil immediately had an idea and joyfully jumped to the other side to dance.

He twisted and turned and after a short while a panda bear emerged
on the paper. Black immediately colored in the areas that needed to
be black. Then Grey repeated the dance, so the first panda was not
alone. Both pencils giggled and squealed, while muffled noises could
be heard from the next page.

It was the crayons groaning and moaning when they saw the pandas. They didn't know any animal that was black like a shadow. Besides, no one wanted to see such a scary animal. And anyway, the lines were much too messy and the black areas too dark.

Annoyed, the crayons left a stain on their way out of the exercise book that was so big, no sketch could fit on the page. But Pencil simply turned the page quickly. He was in a good mood and preferred to dance than look at stupid colored smears.

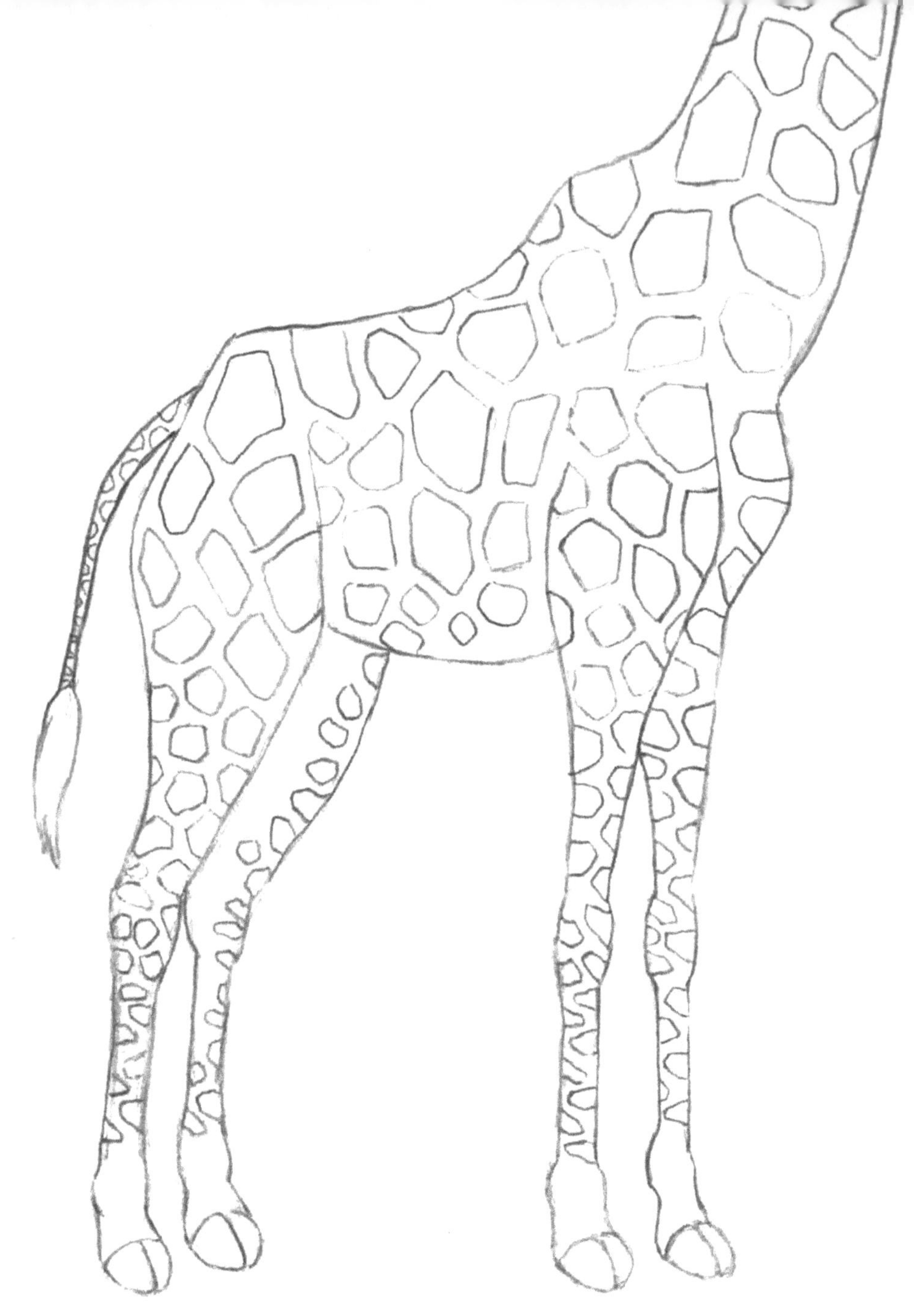

During his next dance, however, he forgot to pay attention to the size of the dance floor. So, without missing a beat, Pencil completed his dance on the next page. But the crayons were already waiting there and tried to spoil Pencil's fun again.

They only saw the bad things and accused Grey of not knowing his boundaries. But this time, Pencil countered their argument - as pencils do - with just three words: a drawing competition! He told them that if he lost, he would only do math for the rest of his days. But if he won, the crayons would agree to color in his drawings.

While he was explaining, Pencil drew the competitors: the crayons against Pencil. But he did not know how to write down the rules. He had learned numbers as a language but had never spelled a word. Anyway, all they needed to know was that Eraser would decide which drawing should stay.

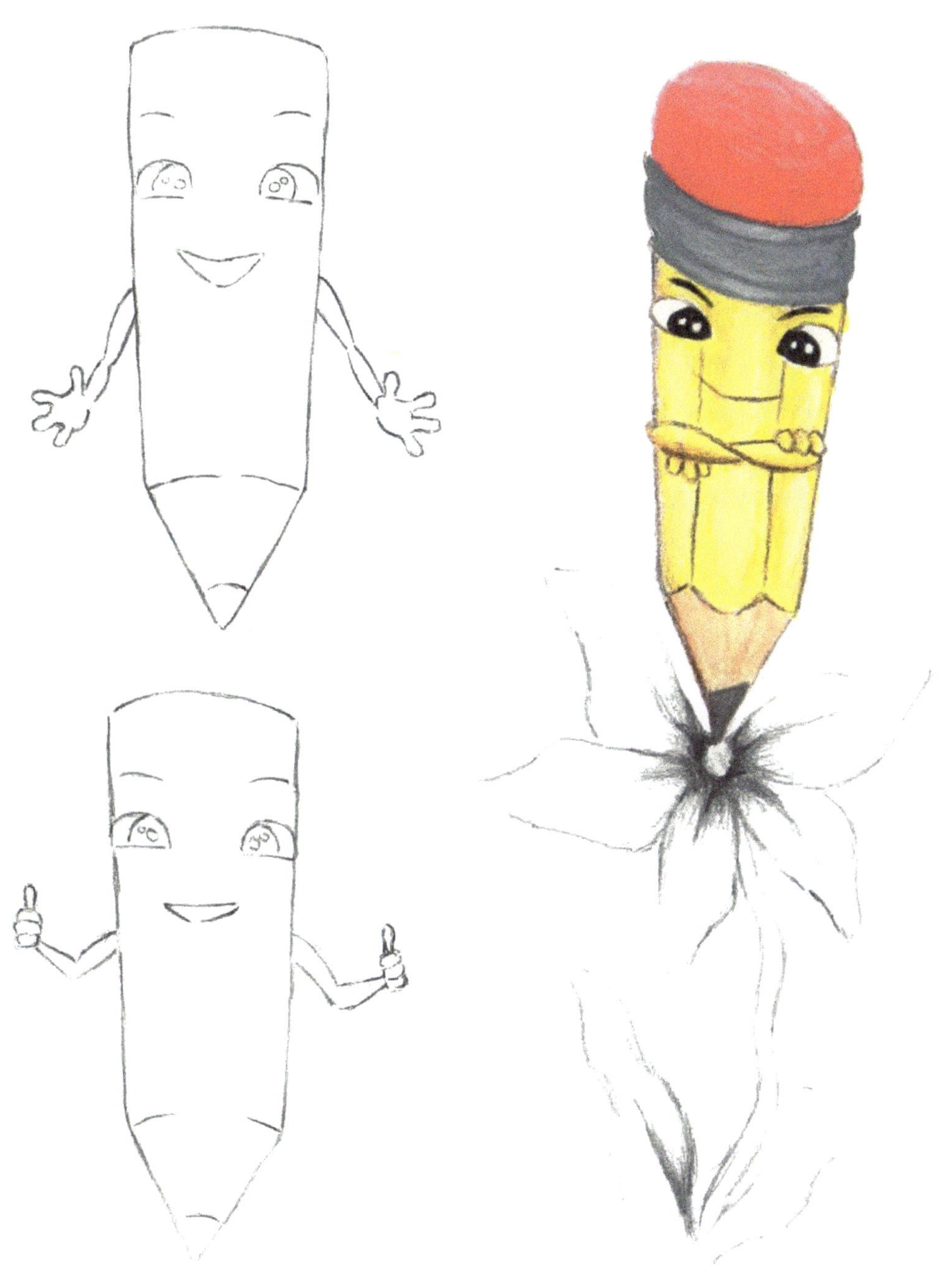

The participants would each be given two blank pages to practice on and the best of three rounds would win. While the crayons were still thinking about which motif to dance, Pencil had already covered all of his dance floor.

The colored crayons couldn't think of a motif on their own, so they tried to copy Pencil's drawing. But they only danced around wildly with everyone drawing where they thought was best, while those who weren't participating cheered from the side instead of helping or guiding the others.

When the crayons couldn't think of anything for the second page either, they asked Ruler and Triangle for help. They were bored because no other pencil could write numbers and note angles. So, they helped the colorful ones make some straight lines. They then called it 'line-ar-t'.

Finally, the practice pages were filled and it was time to meet for the competition. However, doing as crayons sometimes do, they tried to practice on more than just two pages. Pencil took it easy, only determining that the crayons had to get the judge out of her drawer.

Eraser didn't know what was going on when the crayons suddenly picked her up and explained to her about the competition. Usually, others told her where to re-white the pages. Now, she was supposed to decide on the erasing herself, and she didn't want to do that. She preferred to relax in the shade and besides, she had just been asleep.

Eraser watched annoyed as the crayons began the competition with a landscape drawing. It was beautifully colorful and had everything a landscape needed: mountains, trees, clouds and even a small lake. Then it was Pencil's turn.

With a few grey strokes and dots, Pencil created clouds, plants and a small stream. Eraser then decided that both drawings were equally as good. Or maybe she just didn't want to work because she thought that would wear her down.

For the second round, Pencil started. He made a great effort and danced like never before. He squealed so loudly that even the touch-up pen, who usually just lay around giggling, marveled at the great dance from the pencil case. The grey one created a horse, which he called Drab. Then he stared intently at the next page.

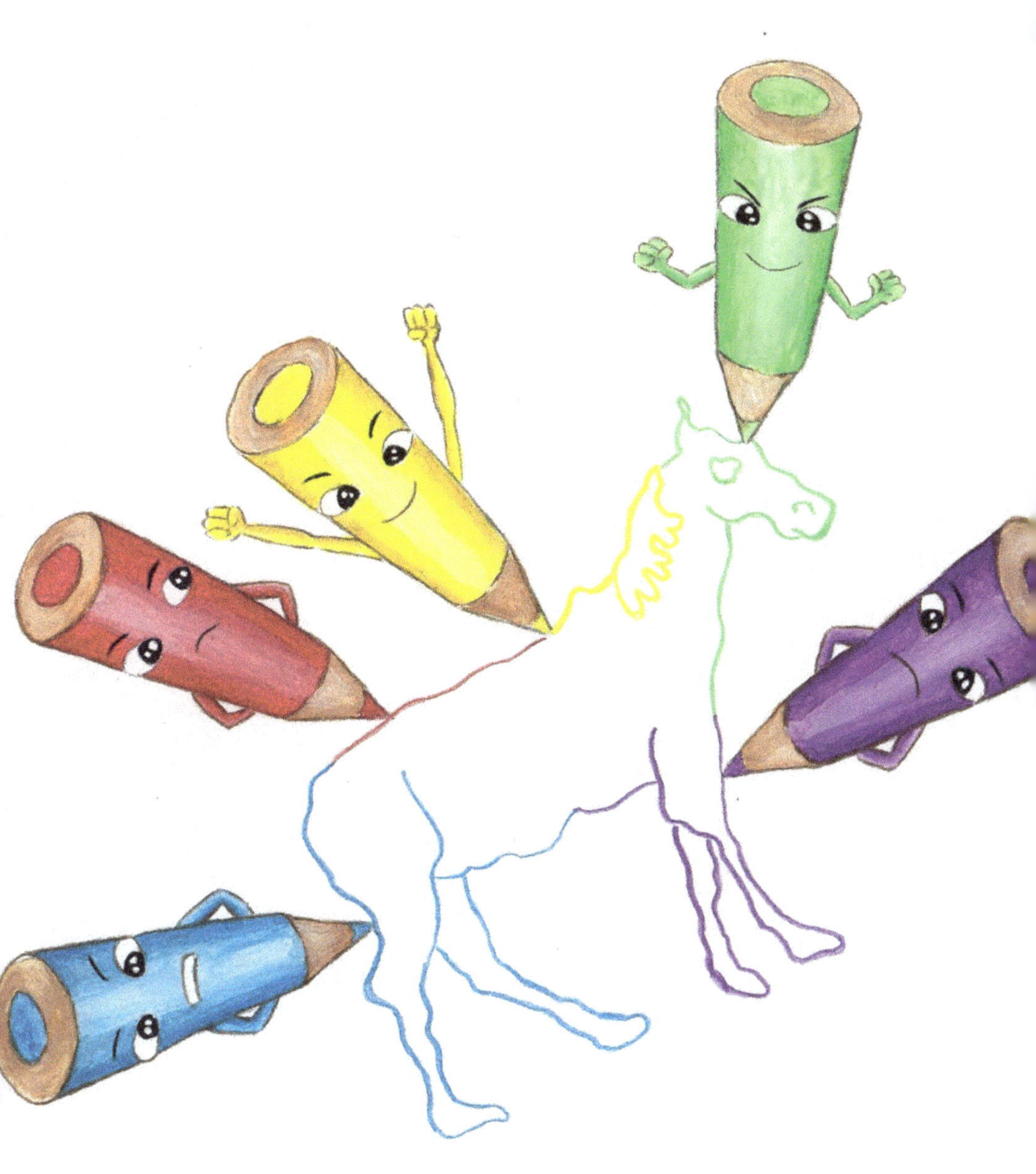

The crayons had, of course, improved due to the practice round. They wanted to win and so traced Drab as accurately as possible. Then they waited for Eraser to decide. However, she had stealthily disappeared and was probably lying somewhere in the shade again. Thus, Pencil eagerly started the third round.

With great attention to detail, Pencil created a lion with a bushy mane.
This impressed the crayons because they didn't know how to draw hair.
But they also didn't want to admit that they had lost, so they said
nothing. However, Black had also been watching from the pencil case.

The coloreds puzzled over what was special about this lion and while they whispered amongst themselves, Black sidled up to them and explained loudly what the crayons had not understood: shades. Being a neutral color, he then decided that Pencil had won!

Since amazed pencils always follow the rules, the crayons accepted the grey one's victory. In addition, the colored ones started to color Pencil's drawing. In the process, one could see that they knew no boundaries and danced across the lines. But the crayons started to realize that coloring in was fun, although first attempts are often difficult.

Pencil showed them some of his dances and with each new drawing the crayons got better. A few pages further on, Pencil prepared a sketch for everyone, and since each crayon knew how to perform the dances by then, something great happened that was to create a togetherness on the desk.

Pencil sketched an animal, but since he himself did not know which stripes to color in, he asked for Black's help. However, before starting, he told Grey that Ruler was mad at him as he had added some letters to a math problem that was on a piece of scratch paper.

Pencil was amazed when he heard that Black could write letters! Apparently, he had learned to write at school when Ink Pen had rolled out of the pencil case and under the bed and had been there ever since. He was blue-blooded, but hardly anyone liked the otherwise hollow pencil.

Pencil only had to ask, and Black helped him with a story about his previous drawings. But the only story that fit the drawings was how they had been created. So, while the crayons were coloring in, Black wrote the words. He called the story 'Painting Black' and needed help from Eraser every now and then.

The crayons drew mice, a sailboat and a butterfly. One day, however, when Eraser had been lying in the sun for too long, she mistakenly erased most of what was on both pages. But instead of being angry, the colorful ones were happy that there was now new space for more

Over time, a simple sketch became ...

... a colorful drawing. That was the prelude to countless children's books that the pencils and crayons created together. The pictures were always colorful, but Pencil's sketches could still be seen. All the pencils and crayons liked the fact that they now worked together. Ruler and Triangle, however, had a different opinion. They had nothing to do now except homework!

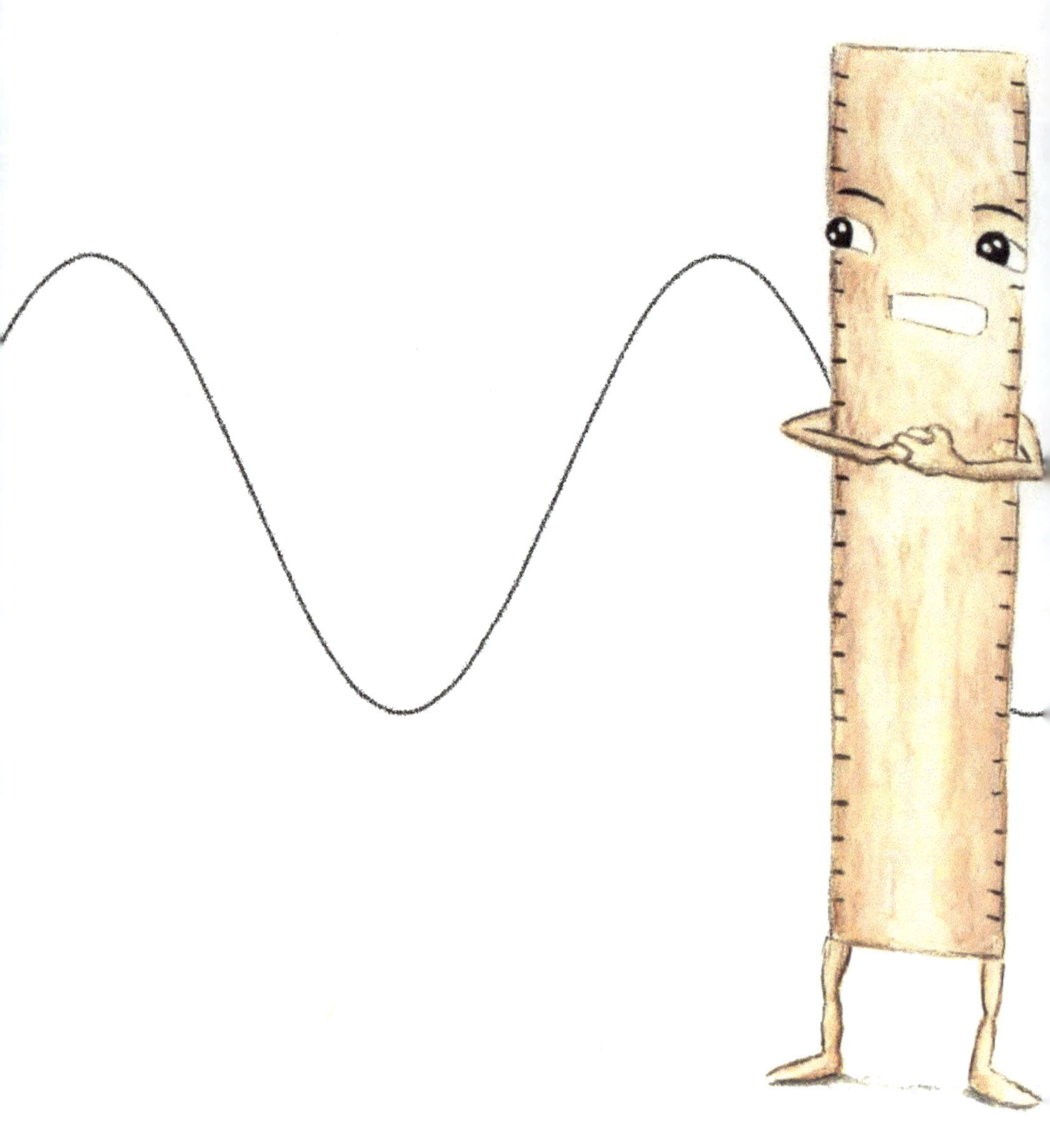

Ruler was particularly angry with Black. Since he had added letters to a math exercise, there were now curves and fewer straight lines to draw. No matter what he tried, Ruler could not bend over backwards. Nevertheless, when he saw how much fun the pencils were having, he also wanted to join in. So, he forgot his anger and from the third page on he helped to write the letters in a straight line.

Triangle joined on page four and helped to place the letters at right angles. Finally, Pencil sketched the colored pencils on the front of the purple booklet. The crayons looked forward to coloring in the cover. Then Black put the title of the story in the name box and summarized on the back what the book was about.

When everything was finished, everyone agreed that together they had created a real book from drawings in an exercise book. It was for children and showed them that they should follow their dreams, even if it was not yet clear when or how they would become a reality. After all, with the help of others anyone can do anything!

There was some space left at the back of the book and there the children could continue the story themselves. It didn't matter if they drew and colored houses, animals or landscapes. The most important thing was that the pencils and crayons could dance and squeak because that's what they liked to do best and what made them happy.

Other books from the desk:

Black has created a rhyming story about a caterpillar stuck in its cocoon. Nevis from "Being Happy with Nevis" is unhappy because of his situation, but he learns that you should make the best of it in order to be happy.

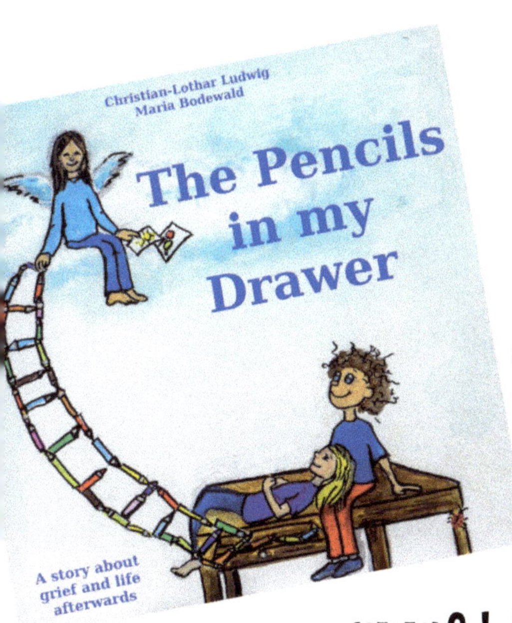

After Pencil danced a dinosaur, the crayons pondered: "How do Dinosaurs Sleep?" Whether what is described in the book is really the case and whether pencils should be trusted with such questions is something everyone has to decide for themselves.

Sometimes sad things happen, but they are part of life. Black came up with a story that helps children experience something difficult or traumatic. Crayons called the story "The Pencils in my Drawer" and made a version for children who miss their mom and their dad.

www.C-L-LUDWIG.com